ALL TOLD

DATE DUE

FEB 2 3 2006			

2004

ALL TOLD

HETTIE JONES

Hanging Loose Press
Brooklyn, New York

Published by Hanging Loose Press, 231 Wyckoff Street,
Brooklyn, NY 11217-2208. All rights reserved. No part of this
book may be reproduced without the publisher's written permission,
except for brief quotations in reviews.

www.hangingloosepress.com

Printed in the United States of America
10 9 8 7 6 5 4 3 2 1

Hanging Loose Press thanks the Literature Program of the New
York State Council on the Arts for a grant in support of the
publication of this book.

Cover painting: *Birthday* by Elizabeth Murray,
Courtesy Pace Wildenstein

Cover design by Ben Piekut

Some of these poems first appeared in *Blueline, Hanging Loose,
Local Knowledge, Ploughshares,* and *The Boston Phoenix.*

Library of Congress Cataloging-in-Publication Data

Jones, Hettie
    All told / Hettie Jones.
       p. cm.
    ISBN 1-931236-20-8 (cloth) -- ISBN 1-931236-19-4 (paper)
    I. Title.

PS3560.O485 A78 2003
811'.54--dc21
                                                    2002032903

Produced at The Print Center, Inc. 225 Varick St.,
New York, NY 10014, a non-profit facility for liter-
ary and arts-related publications. (212) 206-8465

CONTENTS

For Helene

IN DREAMS BEGIN
RESPONSIBILITIES

Genuflection to the God of Lost Gloves

Dear God, I'm truly grateful for my small
red car, my thirty-year-old
washing machine, and my kitchen table's
          extra leaf

As for the rest—

          like the leather glove
                      lost among the literati—

may it serve to remind that only in giving
have I ever found a future
to transfigure the flesh I can never
          fathom

Here, I've tried to say, with my hands full, take
          that I may be revealed

Oh God of Lost Gloves, I'm on my knees, and here
          is my bare hand

Five on the Left Hand Side

Bob Dylan and Queen Victoria
    born the same day
        ditto for
Marilyn Monroe and Cleavon Little

    yesterday Cole Porter, today Judy Garland!

Numerous admirable left-handers
    conspire in my sinister ambitions

        Our labors require
        experiment and the risk
        always
        of failure

In a world of can openers, doorknobs
            shoelaces, screwdrivers

        we learn early to make our
        own ways

        early
        we learn new twists

Name That Tune

if I sing on a rainy Sunday, chances are

I'll go on with any note

I can get my throat

over

I sing a long line

I've sung a long time

I've sung a long line a long time

(repeat)

Accidental Pleasures★

Whenever I hear that song about
   the stairway to paradise
   with its new step every day

I find myself the sole unbeliever
                (eyes off the screen and onto
                   the long thigh of the usher)

So whatever stairs I build have
built-in flaws
               you have to go up one
                               flight
     to get down to another

 it's all
    good clean
            reconnaissance :

mourning dove
the sun at its zenith

nightfall gray as that dove's
lifted wings

he laughed
when I told him
that for breakfast
I had greens although
the knuckles they were
cooked in were tasty as
bacon and with mustard
the sweet black bread

Animal Vegetable

I'm the kind of woman who'll carry
a bouquet of beet greens and expect
              a compliment

  from the newsstand man, who leans in for a sniff,
              but—

They're cold! he protests. Cold greens don't smell!

Well they'd smell if they were growing
              in the warm sweet earth, I cry—
              and out of the corner of my eye, spy
              a stranger lifting the corner of his
                        mouth

Not enough though, I want more—I want
    this Fifth Street jogger, on the run
              from his wife—

      who appears—surprise!
      through a cold wall of green—

      are those for me, he says, are those for
                        me

Self-Portrait As Road Report August 1997

Today I wanted to stay—to stall—
at the Amoco over the interstate

where the land rises and falls
     like breath

          and offers its scars, its
          fresh, deliberate wounds

But then I wanted to leave
and drive the last of summer
on a fast road
              steady
                    into fall

In Dreams Begin Responsibilities★

Stance

What I'm after is the
sight of her face and
the hair I loved braiding

But all I have are
the boxing gloves on our hands

the day they laced us up and faced
us off until we wept at this thirst for
friend against friend for sport

We were six

After that fight
I never fought

The Bike Stops Here

Sixty years and still I feel September evening
coming toward that child of seven, riding
    for the first time unaided

Darkness fingering the trees, the wheels—
    the will commands
    the body understands

★*The title of a 1938 story by Delmore Schwartz, adapted from the epigraph
to* Responsibilities *by W. B. Yeats.*

A Ring Through the Nose

for Nancy Dannenberg

The winter I was nine the War was on
One night we went upstate, to eat
black market steaks in Yorktown Heights

where, unexpected, that first breath
of ice and smoke and oak
thrust—

cut me
open

forever to sharpness, beckoning

forever to the scent of myself, quickening

Liquid Measure, Summer 1952

Nineteen years hadn't readied me

Days in a shack at an Adirondack lake
I made costumes for wealthy girl campers

Nights I found roads to town
until daybreak   astonished me

and diving into that mountain lake
I arrived at a sea change

In troubled water I learned
to trouble the water

In stitch after tedious stitch
I found stroke after furious stroke

19

Dance Dance Dance

In first position: ass tight, legs turned out
    a bird on its own live perch

What a way to hold against cruel
    disappointment!

But missing the ease, slump
    the animal on the earth

~

Sometimes, as if extended, as if *on point*
    the inner self flown all the way out

        observed / observing
        absent / present

I have to snap, shake, shout to get back

Raise this grateful hand to my eyes, count
    one two three four five

Ode to My Nose

Proboscis, you Prominence!

Forgive my every desire to render you
    less noticeable and thus
    more presentable

      —you who proved too much yourself
             to be altered
      who, when I fell and broke your highest bone,
           healed yourself even higher—

Oh ever dependable two-holed eye
my scout to sweet, sour, ripe, rank
    life, death—

Thank you for peony, pine, sandalwood, sage
    coffee, cut grass, honeysuckle, horse manure

    Now I will watch you descend
        toward my mouth
        for a kiss

Modern Maturity

Attitude

S o it's come to this: I'm
O ld. A senior
C itizen, not sure if
I 'm to
A sk for help, or
L ove. But isn't it

S weet that I'll be getting money
E very month? And a subway pass, like a
C hild in school. And I'll walk
U p to the movies and demand my
R ights! As an elder
I 'll insist that all
T ickets must now be mine, half price but
       full view, elder ain't over,
Y ou know?

Anatomy

In the mirror, a
full body frown. The
right breast, always lower
has found its way farther down.

At the curve of that breast
a birthmark they liked.
Now it will have to stay covered.

What strengthens as
the dying body declines?

Action

(*Situp as Zen Flesh Flash*)

over the belly gone to seed go the scarred hands
                    the broken pinky
                        the sliced index finger

                            past the blue and red-
                                veined legs and on
                                        to the as yet
                                            unblemished feet

            goin over to get over

            over and over again

            gettin over the hump

            gettin over the hill

            gettin over the ruin, the hulk

                    the husk   the loss

                        the self

SHOPPING IN DIVERSITY

Scenes from the Life of the Water Towers

in memoriam Denise Levertov

High over the neighborhood
    facing each other in every direction!

    day and night thirst
    the water towers empty and fill
        empty and fill

A woman on a roof counts
      twenty water towers

     their shadows lean
       toward her

Rain hits the water towers
        water inside
        water out

On the roof of the high-rise
    a walled-in water tower, oh

      And the new, unfinished, roofless
             water tower's
       sweet still raw wood

The woman hanging her wash
    clouds running away

Hare Krishna Haute Couture

The hare krishnas hang their robes
    on the fire escape
    of the first tenement
    on Fifth Street

    where, years ago,
    an old man hung out
    his huge cotton underdrawers

until—late every night—he began
    to shout: "PO-lice! PO-lice!
    po-LICE! po-LICE! po-*LICE!*"

    and his neighbors woke, pounding
        and protesting

    and the PO-lice finally came
        and took him away

I hope when they come for me
I'll be shouting something else

        ~

Sometimes, while their robes dry
the hare krishnas
sit reading on the fire escape

shaven devotion
behind pale orange cotton

    as it flies in the wind and the
        complex history

    of those of us who offer up our
        bloomers to the city

Due Canzones

For the Traffic Light at 10th and B

Holding hands with his little sister
Twinned caution, they stand

                              looking
this way, then that. Until she
steps with him off the curb and crosses,
decorous in her skirt, to the other side

where they stroll on, still joined, their
      small hands so willingly
                              swinging

Photo Op With Caption

Middle-aged and full of beans behind their wire-rims,
herewith our "Latin Music Potentates," rulers
      of twenty-first century Latin music

Let its notes hold their smiling eyes   *cha-cha*
      and lay them out on the beat   *cha-cha-cha*

Shopping in Diversity

Copies

Over the counter, in English and Bengali
we talk children, and working mothers' hours
I knew her as a girl in love, braid past her ass
Sometimes her husband's surly on his feet
        at ten at night

I ask if their sons play together
he says they fight together
but she says
        when they *do* play, ah—
    her soft hand flies
    and comes to rest
    on her soft breast

        Cheese

        The Big Cheese has become a Buddhist
        and studies in a little store where once

        another man lived and painted
        and his woman had a hard time
        but she loved him till he died

        The Big Cheese exits today
        with a lanky blonde unlike
        his wife, who is plump from cheese
            and other probable cause

        But isn't she the pillow
        on which he rests his dharma head?

        or is it the blonde, the Buddhist
        and has he fled his life in cheese?

Shoe Repair

with us it's serious—politics
and religion and quotations
over the leather and the rubber
and the machines that whine off
all the doubtful edges
to this perfect, hard shine:
    our compromise

Groceries

Her vegetables fresh, her lipstick too
she says the news is just a distraction
from what's important, which is *us*,
    she says, you and me!

But how to choose between her and *him*!
    A few blocks away, he says
      I'm single
            when I ask
    to buy a single one of his
        two-for-a-dollar
          Asian pears

Cold Snaps

Working toward the winter moon—
　　street crews shoveling slush
　　　　on the dole
　　　　in the cold

　　past me and my unlimited rage

　　　　Coasting on icy asphalt, the bus
　　　　　Taxis skitter like little fish

　　　　Below us, remarkable stilled
　　　　　　complexities

　　　　　and the rats

Snow blurring Amish hex signs
    confounding good and evil

pure snow streaking the sky over Amtrak

    and all of us on the lookout
    for any god in the shape
       of redemption

    A young mother of muffled children
    the bearing that has come to bearing up

    Never pet a dog, it might snap at you,
       some guy says
    Like a woman, he says, you never know
       when she will snap

The Month of July 1991 for Andrew Simpson

Andrew you missed
the total eclipse of the sun
these amazing hot days
    the ozone alert
    the sounds of my saw and
    my hammer, paint smells

Andrew you moved right out of this house
    and into Mother River's cold bed
        gave her your death

        But we
had your life, Andrew
your sound on the stairs
body bump body bump body bump
slam that door
laugh   *eheh eheh eheh*

Andrew you missed
all this heat and then
tonight's rain

but of course now
you are the rain

        and the sun and all that
        no one can ever be
        nothing

We should have told you
this life was enough

October Journey 10/7/99

Why not include getting lost in the Bronx?
October you're so *mean* to drivers—

      all those portents, the afternoon dark's
          third-act curtain—

                                    Show's over, folks,
               time to go—   Home? Out?

      The choice is never clearer to those
      stuck on upper Broadway, going
the wrong way on the wrong day of the wrong month—

October!
        You're the birthday of a long gone lover
        You're all these unfamiliar streets
            the chilly shoulders of an early night

October! Even your tenth month name is wrong!

     You're a goner

         in living color

Homework

When Jason my neighbor suggested I water the street tree
I claimed to be unready to extend my sphere of influence

Jason died in his homemade rope and tire sandals
        fell off a cliff in Australia

The tree that outlived him died too
        of old age and liquidated auto parts
        neglected to the last

Oh these disinclined bones
How to equal the future strewn before us?
Was Jason's footwear up against his life?

In place of the old a new tree waves its few, thin branches

        Once, uncovering brick, I found
        charred beams, their smell
        splintered into my hands

        How can a house hide its gravest wounds

        Some nights I carry this question
        from room to room

After the close
of commerce, when the last
auto part has been sold
and the last crust swept
from the pizzeria's
sticky table, and
the parking lot gate
clanks shut, leaving
only the overnighters
and me, facing west, waiting
for comfort or glory

the half-broken, all-purpose
bike tool, pitchfork
        dowsing
down four floors

Sometimes I dream them gone
to release, to wake

to them anew, and there: the
silk bag of stones, patiently the
chair, clothes, insist

Take cover, says
the quilt. Look here, says
the mirror, you lazy you
fearful says the empty notebook, but

Come, I will help if you let me

Say Goodbye to the Little Yellow Building

for Bob Holman on his fortieth birthday

Say goodbye to the little yellow building
    whose south wall sported
        the first surreal mural in New York
        where a hippie dreamed "Rent A Truck"

Say goodbye to the little yellow building
    that faced the far-out sound
        of Ornette Coleman's plastic horn
    saw the Five Spot fall and its foundation
        uprooted
                  the way they turned it
          and churned it underground, oh

Say goodbye to the little yellow building
    with wide eyes everywhere at once—to the north
        south, east, future, past—
                even your wife's, who
    said goodbye to that, goodbye to all that

    Goodbye to the blaze of afternoon sun
    that shines past the little yellow building
        and falls down the stairs in my
        kitchen like gold soup

    that picks out the pinks in tenement bricks
        and lights dull windows for five
            exquisite minutes
    clotheslines gleaming in far, dusty corners

Say goodbye to that now, pass it, say goodbye
        to the toss and topple of twenties
          and thirties, face
Front! Face up to it! Face the *new* music!

The large, complex apartment building
That grim, heightened portent of progress

Your fabulous forties!   Your first
            fearsome face-off
            with life—and death!
                  And win!
            Win forty more years!

Say goodbye, my friend, to the little yellow building

Say goodbye to the little yellow building

Ode to My Kitchen Sink

Main man, you're my support
your two strong legs, your back
forty years against a brick wall

Though you were old when we met,
even a patch of your iron heart
    already showing
                         I thought
nothing of your imperfection
    only of your double virtue:

      One side deep the other
shallow, you've held washboards
weeks of dishes, babies, even me—
ass in the deep, feet in the shallow
      eyes out the window

Sometimes, Sink, you swallow stuff like
lettuce leaflets or those perfectly formed
fetal broccoli florets   Maybe you need

this sustenance more than that caustic cleanser
and oh I must apologize for so continually
washing out your mouth with soap when you're
this perfect older city-living thing I lean on

    waiting for that day the wrecker's ball
      will say enough, one life
      is all you two get

And given others, Sink, ours has been
    a gift

Ode to Union Square

My dear, you're the
ponytail on the drummer (gray)
his answering smile (wide)

      The word union, of what
      great use it is to the language!
      Roget's has twelve different places to go—
          among them identity, agreement, joining,
          alliance, bond—

Look at the drummer and me, a unit
for one fine moment

    where so many swore to strike together

    their unity like this rhythm in the air
        one hand after another

    Is that what the drummer and I
        are doing—unionizing—

Oh my dear square in December
remand us to the past
to remit us to a future

in which we once more
raise our hands together

All the Time in the World

Death, you bastard
        give me back Dennis Charles!

Don't make me leave him on St. Marks Place
        in his overcoat and his happiness—

            exactly where I left Albert Ayler!

      Is that a stop on the way to
          music heaven?

Dennis, I hope you got there
send my regards—but now

I see how we all share
the very same twenty-four seven

until we fall off just what I wish
        I could offer you—

all the time   in the world

AT THE MIAMI VICE
REST STOP

The Word *Holy*

In those moments, returning
to heat, to the beat
of your excellent heart

returning to the moving blind
against the window—

    this I *now*—

Who can claim holy? I
could have covered my hair, thrown
my wild self to the *mikvah*

But there was always this wet light shaking
its fingers, the self stunned and emergent
the door, the chair, the weight
of miraculous arms, the one
holding me

At the Miami Vice Rest Stop

for Janine Vega

I'm headed for the bathroom
in your shirt, the one your brother
gave you (now he's dead). Miami Vice
is printed on the shirt and it's got
paint and sweat stains and it's thin
and perfect for this weather. I think
of you with thanks — despite your protest
I'll return it.

Miami Vice? you asked. Your brother
    raised an eyebrow

Just like him the rest stop's
on its way to being something
    far from what it was

Two guys eating watch me pass.
The sun is hot, the shirt so old
and yet its legend gets these guys
       their eyes
       meet mine, Mi-
       ami Vice

Note

Dear Marvin Gaye,

I am grateful

for the songs you sang

into our bones, the times

you shook spirit into flesh

flushed us out of our holes

and held us in thrall in your

own hot hungry arms Marvin

Dinner in the Diner

1

for W. S.

In the diner they always play music's
equivalent, a little easy listenin'
but now *California Dreamin',* the original
version, and you are walking toward me
in your Ninth Street apartment
naked and laughing and I am there
thinking you just what I need
to replace all I've lost, you could be
my future. I don't know that
you'll vanish, that someone will say
but I won't believe that you're dead.
No one warned me that music would outlast
the moment it moves, that death and disappearance
are one. But here with my head in my old scarred
hand I'm pulling you back, with you in my arms
I'm climbing the ladder to life

2

Behind me, in the back booth
a man and woman discuss
        her mother's cancer.
She has her list, and he
        his expertise. I listen
        but he's cagey and he's not
                giving it away free

Unlike the girl in the booth ahead—
        "We're having a sexual relationship"

her words float out and it's life over death
                and me in the middle
                        of my pea soup

3

The hair of one patron
is parted in back, as if
by the wind or a do he planned
and forgot. Other than that
he's BLT on toast and tweed.
But blue dusk gleams, the
night's as quick and black
as a swamp, and oh his arms
might be warm

Phone Sex for Race and Gender

Hello, she says.
Hello, he says, there is a wandering colored person
    under your window shouting, and no one
        has heard.
Oh sorry, she says. And this person, uh, just what color
    is it?
Black, he replies fiercely. A black *man*.
Really, she says, you never will fix your glasses. He is
    much more colorful to me. Can't you see his blues,
    his greens, the long white arc of his multicontinental semen?
Oh come off it, he says (idiomatically).
I'd be happy to, she answers.
Cocksucker, he says (familiarly).
Just throw me the key.

Two for the Four A.M. First Snow Show

It's lucky to see first snow he says

diving cold into
the bed, peeling

        the old woman's layers,
        long underwear, afghans
        that hat flies   off

and by what luck, by what trick
        does she unfold,

                miraculous!

             a forced flower
             to the lucky winner

             It's a lucky winter

             Jack Frost's on fire!
             Jack Frost's on fire!

It's lucky to see first snow he says, it's

        lucky to see it he says
        lucky to see it he says
        lucky to see it he says

            melting....

Minor Domo

Fixing the siding I learned,
under one man's eye, illusion

how to nail straight a warped board
bend a straight one to cover flaws

in the house in which we sometimes lived

Not much longer after that we parted

left a perfect skin
on a house that couldn't stand

That Old Man Wouldn't Tell

I asked him how to get old
but he never told

all he said was consider the past
and come to bed

but history's a lie, I wanted the future—
    a vision of that final fall of illusion
        that precedes the cheerful optimism
            necessary for death

    how do you leave it when you are
        so used to gettin it?
    do you take it to the streets?

like the woman works my corner
has to be sixty, her new wig
is it or not economics

she has the whole neighborhood
wondering

Waste Not Want Not

begin with the waste
of kisses, the never-
ending lips and
tongues

then show through
the waste the want
showing its ass

climbed into bed and shook
the beams   maybe try the word
            blame, love, whatever

words tried and found wanting

words that never put cherries
in the wrong man's mouth

end with his wet red lips
and how you want them

April

one robin, one yellow willow
love braving the rain on the wrong highway—
honestly, I don't know what to think!

a Canada goose, a headlong cloud

Open the window!
under my hand, your wet skin
you looking?

thirty April mornings

one white tulip, one red

one precise interior
one persistent stem

~

cherry blossom, silver bridge

don't ever take my sweet
for weak

peaches! peaches! April
has no way to get there yet

quiet room, roaring sky

April, I'm almost over you
    again

THE REAL BROOKLYN DODGERS
ARE FROM QUEENS

Proper Gander

for Kellie and Lisa

One of those girls in the Benetton ad
is loved   by a guy
who
         every time she passes
            larger than life
            on the side of the bus

is amazed and again enraptured

I too am in the Benetton ad
       to the left of
       the boy with the yellow
       lines
            on his face. You might
            not see me unless
                you love me

       but I'm there and the two to my left
            are my daughters, and I

can sure see them, we're
       some lineup
in the Benetton ad
            with all the rest of you
                summery New Yorkers

like the bus, every time
I leave I come back
       to loving

The Real Brooklyn Dodgers Are from Queens

for ChuckDaddy, MamaJ, and Gracie

Losing is hardest after
    you've won some—
        then found the flag
    just out of reach

The trick is to see yourself safe
    on first, fans in the stands,
        all of you breathing
            the next sweet season

Brooklyn Sugar★

might have been the way
they made me. At least
I hope it was sweet, though
she once told me she could
take it or leave it. But she never
did leave, nor he. They stuck like
sugar spilled and left to crust,
which was all I ever saw and always
wondered how it started. Surely
something must have been tasty one of those
nights she wanted to take it, and got
a little sugar in her bowl
a little Brooklyn sugar in her bowl

★*A Bronx sugar distributor*

Back on the Brooklyn Queens Expressway

the girl
who watched the trains
at the end of her block

the one who caught a line and learned
to ride it

When she visits in the middle of the night
do you offer her a hand or a hot meal

Does she accuse you
Do you think she
loves you

now that you've
taken her name and the
shoes she paid cash for

~

she's one of *those*

I cringe when I see her wearing
my clothes

I'd buy her a ticket
but she holds the joystick

she's the one
who enters and leaves

Heirloom Brooklyn

Sarah Lewis boards sailors, one by one
into the parlor turned bedroom. At night,
when the baby cries, she tries to avoid
    the creaky floorboards

in Bay Ridge, Brooklyn, 1902, where sailors
are a fact of Sarah's life since her husband
    left for Newark
Blue-eyed men eating her kasha and kügel
salt red hands on the table

Sarah dies in Bay Ridge, 1926, before
    her baby becomes my mother
    who says I have her mother's
        hands

So I am Sarah banking the fire
as the candle flares and the man appears
the night and a continent
    behind him

and Sarah in daylight, pulling from the bag
    he leaves
this foot-square canvas sky, on which two beaded,
shimmering, smiling, mother/child angels
    fly

and Sarah's hands are mine and her hot heart
    steaming through the Narrows

Letters

Hide

Mother, your glass beads don't shine
in their leatherette boxes.
Silent lie your summer blues, your hot
anxious reds. I'm for plainer
raptures, Mother, but I save yours
and sometimes, in the light, I
run them through my fingers.

April 1999

Friday, Mother, you'll be ninety-seven—eighty-one alive,
sixteen since you died. That day I'm getting a poetry prize,
so we'll have a double celebration. At last your jack of all trades
has mastered one.

Lately, driving to a job, I've passed and repassed the Brooklyn
yard where you stood for a photo with your grandmother
Rachel. You, slender, eighteen, smiling, she noncommittal in her
shetl. All that's missing from this picture is the address, which
you never thought to tell me, and I never thought to ask.

But I'm still questioning your threat—that I'd remain a jack—
and why I took it so to heart. Was it something you saw in me
that I refused to see? This and other questions remain. I'll never
know the address of that place in Brooklyn, nor you how long
I've held on to your warning.

Extending Family

Second Cousin Twice Removed, 1950s

She was never more than
a raised eyebrow

having left three squares
for a full mouth, a studio/apartment
                    an easel and oils
            a window opposite
        a studio couch to fall into

        after the night had fallen
        into the painting on the easel

Somebody's daughter become
    "glancing reference"

From the building where she lived she
        could have seen me set
        my suitcase down

but I never found her

        Cups

        Miss Pearl, before she died, said
        she didn't have to cook every day,
        not since she'd started to use those
        cups, the plastic ones, you know,
        are good for keeping a decent portion
        of greens. That way, Miss Pearl said,
        she kept her appetite up to eighty-
        three. Do that, she said, don't
        lose that care, alone as you are
        don't count yourself out, as if
        you weren't worth
        a cup of greens

Gunnery Sergeant Oscar R.R. "Flat Top" Lee, U.S. Marines, Retired

for Aunt Cora

Uncle Flat's cotton knit kufi
rounds out his head   His glasses
rest on the bone of his face   He's
tubed and wired, his eyes are deep
his mind is clear, he's almost dead

Here is the kiss I left on his cheek
Here are my still warm lips
in the car going home

Driving the dense maze of loss
sorrow growing in my lap
over the black road, the white moon

Three More for the Road

Highway Praise Song

Praise the quiet horse,
my journey past him

Praise Route 80's lofty silos
every semi gunning for the city

Praise the waitress in the AmBest truck stop
she who never eats a meal
and mystifies her doctors

Praise her red blond curly hair
her rotting teeth, her smile
of recognition

Repetitions, Route 212

first light
first bird's
one slow call
                and into the light
the call and response, the yellow iris
           purple daisy
      red car
    new black asphalt
already broken on the shoulder
      of the road

and beside that road the river

and moving past the moving river
one orange busful of gleeful
children

and then this butterfly
every color already mentioned
already weary of it all, and resting

Sharing the Image

Because Jan imagined the tinker
I forgot to remember
this hill in that blizzard

       the big green Plymouth's
          bald tires

holding myself off the brake
on the Saw Mill River Parkway

As for Jan's tinker, she saw him
       in the desert, his noisy pots
       hung on the side of a car
       that suddenly appeared
       beside him, with no license plate
       its right front window broken

He just came banging into her mind like that

and now into mine

behind me ribbons of light
       unwinding

Rabbits Rabbits Rabbits*

8/1/86

for Harry and Estelle

the first is on the lawn
      the second in a meadow
            the third runs out from under the carport—

        rabbits rabbits rabbits!

next day in the city
a couple helps their toddler
climb the steep steps to a building

           and there you are
          with the hands of a child
       held between you, the live palms
         tender as those animals

* *To ensure good luck for any coming month, say these words*
  immediately upon awakening on the first day.

3/1/87

>Julio, our rabbit
>black with a white chest
>ran free like the rest
>
>ate the hall floor
>and the bedclothes
>
>trained himself
>to the catbox
>
>stuck his head under my hand
>to be petted, and waited
>
>a soft, expectant, rapid
>>heart of silence

And if Julio—may he rest—
then everything furred and feathered
and scaled, even the rough broad leafed
>and thorned

Two for the Proofreader's Lunch

Bates Direct

A long day with nothing to do
but study the walls of the woman
who usually works here. A photo
of her cat, framed and given
pride of place above a snapshot
tacked up with pushpins, a mustachioed
guy in cutoffs and shades. Full head
of hair, nice legs, husband, lover?
Are they away on vacation together?
Has her faith in herself increased
since last year when she pencilled this:

    I'm not a good writer because I'm
    unable to sustain any moments of
    lucidity long enough to write them down.

             or—as I get it—

  can't sustain

            lucidity

  long enough

        to

           write it

I wonder what led her to think
that writing proceeds from lucidity
when it truly begins in the dark.
You start from nowhere, from blood.
You're never sure you'll get there
but you hope. So find the dark first, Alice
and bon voyage.

Uniworld

What if uniworld demanded uniword?

How to choose when they're all so tasty
    in the mouth's wet machinery

Speech is like food, take *salt,* for example
    curling the tongue, or *rock*, locking
        the glottis

      even the toothy, urgent stutter of *it*
        as in *rock it,* baby

And doesn't salt need sweet, and don't
    both lie next to hot, like making love
    in summer, the salt sweet sweat
        of it?

Call it love then, or sleep, or night or
    mist or rain, but speak its
        rightful name

Bon Voyage for Eric for Love of Life and the Loan of Larousse

for Eric Richards

Without tomorrow *a deux—adieu*!
I'll give you my yesterday *seule:*

                    a starfield over a snowfield
                    slashed by a dark line of road
                    I first took for a river

I can imagine a running river
one where we might stand
        on the bank

                    but this is the season of
                    champs de neige, of
                    patient trees and
                    one soul *seule* with them

                    auditeur, ecoutante
                    je veux entendre
                    un autre monde

Hettie's Hex for Fee

in memoriam Fielding Dawson

This is Fee's sixtieth birthday

> (a line in dactylic hexameter
> a six-footed Greek mode, as in Homer)

though plainsong goes straighter
goes "like sixty" (definition 5):

> "with great speed, ease, energy, or zest"
>   as
> *Everyone was working like sixty to finish
> up before the holidays.*

Still you can't take the six out of sixty

> the sixth sense is intuition

> the sixth man on a basketball team
> —its "best substitute"—plays every position

> and a six-wheeler, in CB slang, is a small
> truck, which is really large and perfectly echoes

the derivation that traces sixty
from *sixtig* to *zestig* to *sechzig* to *sextigir* —

What have we here? sex tiger!

And him a sixty-year-old man!

Peter Pinchbeck's Missing Metaphor

for Daniel

Peter was the star of the party

Even though he had died
he was seen and heard again
came to life, as it were

And it was, since in a video Peter
came to the life where we had been
talking and drinking and toking

until we fell silent watching
Peter in full, reassuring color

But then he vanished, left the party
just like that before the credits

and his son stunned, pinned to the couch
grieving this *likeness*

What is *like* life?

GLOBAL WARNING

Global Warning

You want to look hard
at the first hard rain
after a drought

      Watch it drench the pizza guy on his bike
            set him awash in his dangerous life

      It'll put you in your place
            if you're lucky enough to have one

You want to look hard at this rain
and know it means business
and that your business

      is to feel it, feel the sky
      giving way giving life giving water

"The Doorman Has Been Paroled"*

for Jan and Precious

I caught her out of uniform
    and would have stopped
        to pick her up
except for being on my way
    to all the doors she'd left

where more than many doormen
      take her place

New Southern Exposure**

Garbage at the shore below the levee

Levee holds—and hides—the muddy Mississippi
with its chemical effluvia

Acid in the rain, in the pipes that cross the road,
in the pesticides and herbicides, and in the fields
the greens

On the greens the grainy feel   Feel it on your
fingers   Eat it on your lunch tray   Eat it

in an ante bellum or a shotgun house
beside the local prison

where the keepers too are kept
and all that changes is the product

* *Notice in a prison classroom under "Close This Door."*
** *Special Counsel to the Justice Department, on the problem*
   of where to put our prisoners: "It's sort of like hazardous waste."

Air Jamaica

The Bull Bay road runs paved
until good intentions run
into dust and weeds and goats
    and feral dogs
                 where all is
broken—house, tree, promise—
and more is coming when it comes
to mangoes grown on good will only

    Who stole
the water? Who bought up the green ?

    Behold cement plants belching
blocks for those whose home was always
    plum, or tamarind

Page from *A History of War*

Alarum
for a girl   being carried
across a street   in Tripoli

by a young man who grips
her rigid body across his own
as he would a gun

a girl stiff with terror, fixed
in the gross heat of her pain
she suffers

as the man suffers
a last, running look at life
the scream he swallows
is a taut swell the same shape
as the girl's screaming mouth

I can see his long, thick jugular
even in this newspaper photograph

I am looking at Saturday night
November 19. Nineteen hundred and
eighty-four approaches as they
approach death

I beg you: smell the blood

For the African Street Boy Celebrating International AIDS Awareness Day 1998

and what will this moment of silence do
that our withheld science has not?

    You are doomed   your life   bought out
        your home   thrown down

           But here   and now

      I take your soft hand   I trace
your lips   the curve
      of your nose   I raise the dead
behind your eyes

      I celebrate their every living bone

      Remember!   Silence Equals Death!

Laments for the Afghan Women

War, Sar Chesma

Where is the ring
he put on her finger
during the time
before this time of
no him, and no house but
this burlap sack with
their bed pad, still faintly
stained with the life he left,
all that is left of him,
the stain the size of the
blot on her heart as
the flatbed truck behind her
waits to receive her, since
the house is dust
like the body that left
the stain, and the truck
is a way to the nowhere of
no house, no him
        and now no ring.

Her empty hand feels weightless
her finger a barely covered bone

Escape, Kabul

A doctor flees to avoid arrest
for attending a luncheon.

I said darling, I said
dear. I said baby,
I said daughter
I am leaving

ask your father to tell you why

why we took photos
why we played music

ask your father
why I'm gone

I said darling I said
dear, I said baby,
I said daughter
there will be no life without you

I said baby there
will be no life, but
I have sworn to do no harm
and so I will not stay for death

Lament for a Turkish Suicide Age 22

What she wanted was more

    school or a job, anyway
    she got herself a tight skirt

She didn't want to live
        hiding herself

But her father burned her skirt
        and then three people
        beat her bloody

She lived just long enough to write
    that she wanted to die

and then she climbed some stairs
        and stepped into the air

        and left
        the fabric of her
        brief life

ALL TOLD

When What You See Is Not What You Get

easy to mistake a light source, take
tenement bare bulb for moony romance

or there's a flash of someone familiar
at the corner until the wind turns

and the dream leaves
your foot twisted, as though
you'd really been in that hole
prove you weren't

don't you often take the heat of your body
for some kind of truth

or mourn the moth that appears out of season
frantic to buzz you and falls, confused by
your batting hands, into your hot coffee

and drowns, is delivered
from shape, from that heat

sometimes you can't tell
whether you're looking at
        life or death

A Nebula of Noteworthy Nellies

for Nellie Engle and for the Nellie
character in a recent literary work

for strength I give you
      Nellie Taylor Ross, the first woman
      governor. Elected by Wyoming, 1925

and for inspiration
      Nellie Monk, wife to Thelonious

and though I'll admit there are nervous Nellies
      and fussy Nellies

Nellie, f.y.i., is a form of Helen, that beauty
      who caused such havoc

and sometimes Helen is confused with *heleane*
      a word describing a planetary aura
      named by sailors for their patron saint:
          St. Elmo's fire

and when two electrical conductors meet
      the air is ionized, changed
      in a coronal discharge
      called St. Elmo's fire

So burn on burn on burn on Nellie

Second Hand Shod

A woman with good taste and small feet
quit Laramie, Wyoming one cold spring
leaving silver leather sandals

A half size too small, the feet of my youth
before life spread me out—I bought them anyway
and, accommodatingly, in time they became mine

That woman must have been on her slow way
east. She ditched New York at the millennium
leaving soft yellow suedes with ribbon ties
(for chilly nights when warmer feet
can better take you farther)

And now she's come and gone again—
she just abandoned red slides—her dancing shoes!
At once I put them to good use

thinking of her, restless as I
when my feet were smaller

and wherever she's stepping
I want her to know I'm behind her

Dust—A Survival Kit   9/11–10/11 2001

9/25

Two weeks breathing the dead

each breath marking each
stunning absence

ourselves as coffin,
winding sheet, urn
worm

but oh, of what is God made?

10/2

We lived among blossoming words
until some of them exploded, like one
human exploding another

say *human* again
try to feel the word
on your lips

10/11

The dead have dispersed.
It has rained on them twice
they have drifted to sea
ascended in mist

Breathe them once again

and begin

Caught, April 2002 — A Prayer for Peace

The Islamic Army
for the Liberation
of Holy Sites

has taken responsibility
for the bombing
of historic Ghriba synagogue
a popular tourist attraction in Tunisia

Let us mark the martyrdom
of Nizar bin Muhammad Nawar
who called his contact in Germany
an hour before the act, to say
"Don't forget to pray for me"

So let us pray within the badly scorched
synagogue, founded twenty-five hundred
years ago by those fleeing the destruction
of King Solomon's temple in Jerusalem

who brought with them one of its stones
rubble from another liberated Holy Site

The Ghriba explosion killed seventeen people
twelve of them German tourists—German?

This poem is unfinished, as are we all,
as is, for now, Jerusalem, holy home to
        Jahweh, Allah, God—
for whom Solomon's stone equals Jesus' cross
equals Nizar bin Muhammad Nawar's vengeance—

and whom we could not, would not kill
so we kill the messengers so that ours, in turn
        will be killed

and we will pray for them
and we will pray for them
and we will pray

Like (as if)

on the lip
of the world's cup
hangs straight talk

so think like this: like (as if)

you're a lucky girl
in a clean bed

    —ah, but will your hands fail
        first, or your heart—

so think like this: like (as if)

you're in the soup
and only in the end
will you have been eaten
        all up

forgive me, Julia Child, I have eaten
the same dinner two nights running

since I have only myself to please
and am pleased by the farmers
of New York State, from whom I buy weight
and with whom I shamelessly flirt

Julia, I am way too plain in my tastes
I like the food itself
more than itself reshaped

tomato slush
the green in the squash
the yellow in the corn
        purple in the dark gleaming sex
        of the eggplant

Julia, I feasted on these while reading the poetry
            —the poetry in the obituary—
        of a man I'd admired

And reading his obit

        obit from the Latin *obitus*, death
                the date of one's death
                to meet one's death

I thought, dear Julia Child, as you might
                                    see it

        a bite today
        obit tomorrow

All Told

to October 13, New York, humor, plants, legs, motherhood and destiny

in memoriam Kenneth Koch

It's warm in New York, my favorite place, and everyone
is hanging out in shirtsleeves or sleeveless, not like
that long ago October day when it was cold enough
for the woolen suit I wore to my first and only wedding—

How lucky I am to have my good humor! Without it I might
have been blue instead of delighted enough with my life
and the two baby house plants I've just brought home
to share with me their destiny, or maybe to combine us
in that one big destiny—

But oh, I've forgotten my legs! How could I leave them out
of such an important poem—and maybe they deserve one
of their own for holding me up all this time through joy and pain—

strong enough to push me through the streets
while my lazy ass sits on its bike seat—

Oh New York, it's Friday the 13th and I haven't even
    mentioned motherhood
but that's another whole story, and all told I'm just as happy to
        end here, wherever that is

with my plants and legs and humor, and all of you and yours
    out there in that destiny we share